CW00857487

EVERYONE'S INESCAPABLE
COMPANIONS CHOICES AND
CONSEQUENCES

EVERYONE'S INESCAPABLE COMPANIONS CHOICES AND CONSEQUENCES

By Billy K. Crawford

Xulon Press

Xulon Press
2301 Lucien Way #415
Maitland, FL 32751
407.339.4217
www.xulonpress.com

© 2020 by Billy K. Crawford

All rights reserved solely by the author. The author
guarantees all contents are original and do not
infringe upon the legal rights of any other person or
work. No part of this book may be reproduced in any
form without the permission of the author. The views
expressed in this book are not necessarily those of
the publisher.

Unless otherwise indicated, Scripture quotations taken
from the Holy Bible, New International Version (NIV).
Copyright © 1973, 1978, 1984, 2011 by Biblica, Inc.™.
Used by permission. All rights reserved.

Printed in the United States of America.

ISBN-13: 978-1-6305-0708-4

CONTENTS

INTRODUCTION:

No matter who you are; or were you live; what language you speak, or were your geographically located. There is no escaping these 2 companions choices and consequences. We all have choices to make each and everyday. What time to get up? What time to go to sleep? What do I eat? How much money do I spend on getting a car or house? Which doctor do I go to etc? The list is endless. I don't think anyone really knows how many choices the average person makes everyday. I know I couldn't tell anyone.

The thing is for every choice there is going to be a consequence. There is no escaping the consequences either. They will come. Some consequences don't come at that exact time the choice was made, sometimes the consequences come days, months, or even years later but you can rest assured they will come nevertheless.

In this book i'm going to talk about choices and consequences and how they affect us all. I'm not a professor, or philosopher, or priest, or politician, or some expert on human beings. I do not claim or never will claim to be wise or perfect person. I am however a human being like everyone else. Who like every other human being and everyone else has been greatly impacted by these 2 companions choices and consequences. It doesn't matter who you are, what you believe or don't believe. Weather your a man, woman, rich, poor, black, white, a King, Queen, Bishop, a leader, or follower, president, congressperson, rich, poor, healthy, sick, or just a common person. What is your title or what do you call yourself or how do you see yourself? Are you a man, woman, child, A hustler, pemp, smart, ignorant brave, fearful, and atheist, religious, christian, budist, muesluem, a scholar, teacher, mechanic, scientist, doctor. What color are you Black, white, brown, red, blue with purple polka dots, none of that makes any difference to these 2 companions. If your human and breath and bleed just like I do you have been and will continue to be greatly impacted by these 2 companions choices and consequences. Just like me and everyone as long as we're all alive. No one I know of, nor have I heard of, or read about throughout the entire history of the human race has escaped these 2 companions choices and consequences. It doesn't matter where you go and what you do these 2 companions are always there. Maybe I'm crazy for asking this but is there anyone anywhere that has escaped these 2 companions choices and consequences please find me i'd like to meet you.

A LITTLE ABOUT MYSELF

———————

I was born in colo in dec of 63. I'm been married now 39 years to the same woman. God blessed us with two kids a daughter and son and 4 grandkids 3 granddaughters and 1 grandson. I've been to college got an associate degree. I've worked different Jobs have a lot of different experiences. I currently drive a truck been all over the United States meet all kinds of people from all over the world from all walks of life and cultures. I have spent most of my life just silently observing people. How they live what they do what they believe and how they feel. I notice something they are all just as human as I am and they are dealing with these 2 companions choices and consequences. This is the first Book that I have written Lord willing I plan to write a series of books on different real life issues and topics. However that depends on the Lord and you readers out there if no one ever reads this first book why write another. I know there are going to be critics, and I know that there will be the non critics. This book is from my own observations over the years. I'm not writing this book to be politically correct because the 2 companions choices and consequences doesn't care about that either. I do hope that by reading this book you can relate to these 2 companions choices and consequences. They are there no matter who you are, no matter what you do, no matter what you say, no matter how you feel, no matter where you live, no matter where you go, Its like that saying and the song Martha and the Vandellas sing there no were to run nowhere to hide. There's no escaping these 2 companions choices and consequences.

Chapter 1
THE 2 COMPANIONS

I am going to devote this first chapter to why I referred to choices and consequences as 2 to companions that we all have with us and can never escape. Now before I begin I want to say a couple of things. 1st most of the things in this book are just my own personal observations and experiences and observations of my life time of the human race and history. The 2nd thing is this for years and years people have tried to deny the existence of God and that the Bible was written by a bunch of men and is just a book of good stories and no way the things God said are true; they are just made up by men especially the beginning of the Bible the story of creation account that God spoke everything into existence. Instead that everything came about by chance and everything has evolved from something else. Well to all that I want to say this Who am I to tell anyone who to believe in or what to believe in. But the more I personally have to deal with these 2 companions choices and consequences the more I'm convinced that the Bible is the true word of God and that he is for real and does exist and is in control. Weather you believe in Jesus (God) or not. Weather you believe the Bible and everything it says is true or not. If your an atheist, or maybe your evolutionist, or whatever you believe in or whoever you believe in. If there is no God and if the Bible isn't true? Then try to explain these 2 companions away. The Bible teaches that out of everything God created that the human race is the most unique because he created the human race with a free will. Other words a right to choose whatever we want. From the most simplest of things to the most complex of things. This is why I'm so convinced that the Bible is true and God is for real. Let me say this; is there anyone who can prove that these 2 companions choices and consequences aren't always there each and everyday of my life and everyone else's. For there to be no God and for the Word of God the Bible not to be true there would not be the 2 companions choices and consequences to deal with.

The 1st companion just presented me with a choice to make. I chose to write these statements just now. The 2nd companion is going to bring about some consequence, or outcome, or result, of the choice I made. Out of these 2 companions what he does and brings is one of my worst fears in life, one thing is for sure his results or consequence will come and they will be either good or bad, dire or beneficial. Now if you have read up to this point you are being dealt with by companion 1 choices you have to make a choice whether or not you should continue to read this book or not. Weather you choose to read the rest of the book or not please take a few minutes and think about the 2nd companion consequences of the choice you have to make.

Now with all that out of the way and if you choose to continue to read the rest of this book let me begin. Now in the Bible in Solomon's Writings especially the book of Proverbs which letters he wrote to his children Solomon refers to Wisdom as a woman. I admire the way Solomon did that it makes it so easy to relate to. So that's why I chose to refer to 2 companions to describe choices and consequences. We are all around people all the time and we can all relate to people in some fashion, shape, or form.

Now I've noticed these 2 companions reveal themselves when were at a very young age. These 2 companions are not invited they are just there. I've noticed these 2 companions are no respecter of person. There is no racism, no prejudice in them. These 2 companions don't care what the color of your skin is, if your male, female, if your young, old, rich, poor, short, tall, what language you speak, even what you wear. I've noticed these 2 companions seem to know everything about us and how we feel at all times. I've noticed that these 2 companions have been around since before the beginning of the human race and will still be here after I'm dead and gone. I've noticed that no matter where I go or what I'm doing the 2 companions are there. They never leave me alone. If I go to the store they are there. If i go to work they are there. The 2 companions are there when I take a shower, when I eat. When I go to sleep, when I wake up. I can be in the air, under the ground, on the water, and the 2 companions are there.

3

I've noticed there is no getting rid of the 2 companions you can't call the police and have them removed and thrown in jail. I can't shoot them, i can't chase them off with a stick there nothing I can do to rid myself of these 2 companions. The 2 companions are there in every situation and circumstance I get into. In everything they are there these 2 companions. What's really unique about these 2 companions that I've noticed is that they are there with everyone else to in all places at all times with all people. These 2 companions choices and consequences is with us all. Oh I have tried to escape from these 2 companions time and time again. But to no prevail there is no escaping them nowhere to run nowhere to hide from these 2 companions choices and consequences. What really scares me the most about this is no one i've seen, meet, or read about in history books, the Bible, the newspaper etc has escaped either. Is there anybody out there alive or dead that has not been impacted by these 2 companions choices and consequences? Oh how I would like to meet them!!

Chapter 2
OTHER PEOPLE'S ARGUMENTS, OPINIONS, & THOUGHTS

Now before I get into this book more about these 2 companions choices and consequences I want to go ahead and address some arguments, opinions, and thoughts about me that may or may not come from people that may read this book. I don't know who will read this book, and how they will react to what I'm going to say in this book. I know there has been other books written about choices and consequences but like this one.

The other books about choices and consequences that have ever been written or will ever be written in the future and this book hasn't by no means said enough about these 2 companions choices and consequences. I don't think anyone can ever say everything there is to say about these 2 companions and put in a book. It would be a never ending book, but that is just my own personal opinion, or you could say my own observation, or view. Once again who am I to tell anyone anything.

I was going to write this chapter toward the end of this book, but after some prayer and thought I choose to write it as the 2nd chapter of the book. I want to make sure that whoever reads this book understands that they choose to read this book, and that all this is from my perspective. I'm not trying to force any of my views on them, nor am I saying that anyone has to even agree with me and what I'm going to be saying in this book. By no means am I claiming to be an expert on people's morals, behavior, mind set, feelings, or anything. I'm simply another human being with my own problems and issues. The one thing I can tell everyone is that I am not perfect. I have shortcomings, downfalls, faults, and I have made some terribly bad choices in my lifetime, and I've had some dire consequences to deal with because of the choices I've made. In fact, this is my first book I have ever written.

Some people that read this book will probably praise me for it and say that I'm real wise. Some will say I'm crazy. Some may say I'm some kind of radical. Maybe some will say I'm some kind of fanatic. Some may get offended. Some may get angry. Some may want to argue with me. Some people may call me out and drag me through the dirt and say all kinds of things about me. I may be called stupid, ignorant, arrogant, and the list goes on and on as to what people can say about me, and what they can do to me, and how they may feel about me after reading this book. Everyone has the right to all their opinions of me. Once again who am I?

I would ask one thing before anyone decides what they choose to think, feel, or do about me and this book. That is this before you do, say, think, anything explain away these 2 companions choices and consequences. The truth of the matter is that they are there. And can anyone escape from them and their impact on the whole world. Every culture, every race, every society. No matter what you believe, no matter where you live, no matter what you do. It doesn't matter if your black, white, rich, poor, a celebrity, a King, a beggar on the street. It doesn't matter if your scientist, teacher, CEO of some big company, a preacher, and atheist, a leader, a follower, man, woman. You and I have to deal with these 2 companions choices and consequences. If you can't explain away these 2 companions? Or you never had to deal with them? If you live in a world where you never make choices and never have consequences from those choices you had to make? By all means be my guest to criticize me, this book, God, the Bible, the universe and everything. You won't get any argument from me. The truth is that these 2 companions do exist and God is the one who put them with us all. Which makes me ask these questions. Are we really alone? Is there really no God? Are we all here just by chance? Do we really have a purpose and destiny in this life? I can only speak for myself. I'm never alone. Yes there is only one God and he is for real. I'm not here just by chance. Yes God created me for a purpose and has given me a destiny. As long as the 2 companions are around choices and consequences no one will convince me otherwise. Once again who am I. Now by this point who ever read this book has to deal with this 1st companion choices. You have to make a choice whether to put this book down or to keep reading it. Either choice you make you will then have to deal with the 2nd companion consequence. I'm having to deal with them both because I chose to write this book, there is no escape for me. Can you escape?

Chapter 3
PREDETERMINED CHOICES

I'm going to devote this chapter to talk a little bit about predetermined choices. I'm not going to speak too much about this because predetermined choices is a topic for one of the next books Lord willing that I am going to write. However I do need to write a little about it in this book. I trying to make sure to cover everything.

Now what is predetermined choices? I'm pretty sure that all of us grown adults and mature adults understand the word predetermined. But I'm not sure that is a safe assumption, so just in case I'm going to define the word predetermined and once again in my own words so it may not be the words out of a dictionary somewhere; remember I said in my intro that all the content of this book was my own personal observations and is not necessarily politically correct.

The word predetermined simply means some choice or decision that was all ready made for me. Other words I didn't get to choose someone or something already choose it for me and there is nothing I can say or do about it or to change those predetermined choses. Here's a couple of examples I did not get a choice in when I would be born. I do not get a choice when I will die. Those choices have already been predetermined by someone higher and more powerful and way beyond me. His name Is Jesus (or God, or the Creator, or what every title you want to use for him). We all have predetermined choices that were already made for us. To bring this thought down to earth and a little closer to home for everyone here are a couple of other examples I hope I will be able to help everyone relate to what I'm talking about here. If you have just recently had a new born baby does the baby decide on which brand of diapers you will buy it at the store. Of course not it incapable of making that choice you as the parent make the choice for them. Another example did any of us get a choice in who is your mother or father when we were born. We all only have 1 biological mother and father. These are all predetermined choices. And yes there are consequences on these predetermined choices also.

I hope some of you by now are beginning to see these 2 companions how much they impact us all in such a great way. The 2 companions are always there how can I escape them? If only I could eluded them for even 1 second, 1 min, 1 day. But I can't get away from them even when I have had predetermined choices made for me if I had been given choice I may have and probably would have chosen something different. I want to ask this question? It just doesn't seem fair does it? But when has life ever been fair!!!

These 2 companions even impact us and affect us all even with all those predetermined choices that are made. We still have to deal with them no matter what. I like to say again out of the 2 companions the 2nd one consequence is the one I fear most of all because even when there are choices made for us a lot of times we have to deal with the consequences of choices of others. The 2 companions aren't going to let me off the hook that easily. What about you?

Chapter 4
HISTORICAL ACCOUNTS OF THE 2 COMPANIONS IMPACTS AND OUTCOMES TO US ALL

———————

Well i hope by now you all are still with me. I'm going to start getting into the meat of this matter as I said I would earlier. What better way to start than with history. Your suppose to give footnotes telling about your references and quotes that you use that are from someone else or from some other resources that you may use in a book that you are writing. But since I'm not going to be quoting things word for word and since my references are going to be pretty general I'm not going to use footnotes. Not only that but now days with the internet and technology the way it is anyone can go look these things up in detail by the click of a button. I'm not going into a bunch of details just general info. I guess another way to put it is a lot of paraphrasing. I chose to do it this way for the sake of time and so I don't have to have some million page book.

Let's see where do I begin? There so many impacts and outcomes from these 2 companions. I wonder how different things would have been in our world today had the Roman Empire had made different choices and not spread themselves out to the point that they couldn't govern everything like they could have. History tells us that choice is what lead to the downfall of that Great Empire. What would've happened if the people of the Roman Empire had chosen different people in power or authority. Companion 1 presented them all the choices the right ones and the wrong ones. That's one of the unique things about companion 1 he has all the choices. Another way to put is that he presents to us all every kind of choice known to the human race and he never has a shortage of them. Companion 2 brought about his consequences for the choices the people of the Roman Empire made. The ultimate consequence was the downfall of a nation. For every choice there is a consequence there is no escape from these 2 companions.

What would of happened if the North and the South would have chose to agreed on the issue of slavery? Or would have chose to abolish savery? Weather they would have agreed to abolish slavery or to keep it. Had the North and South chose to agree on the same resolution on the issue of slavery there would of never been a Civil War and we would of never had all those men die. There wouldn't have been father against son, brother against brother; and there wouldn't have been a divided nation. Once again companion 1 presented all the choices right and wrong. Once again companion 2 brought about the consequences from the choices that were made. The ultimate consequences was a nation that end up divided and more men dying in that one war than in all the other wars in our nation's history. There is no escape from the 2 companions.

What would've happened had the China dynasty would have choose not to build the Great Wall and would have opened up all its borders instead. Once again companion 1 presented all the choices right and wrong. Once again companion 2 brought about the consequences of the choices that were made. The ultimate consequences was that Lots of men were killed building that Great Wall a lot of them were buried alive during its construction; and the price of building that Great Wall cost them more than just money and resources it was paid for with a lot of blood. There is no escaping these 2 companions!

I just gave 3 basic general examples of the impacts of these 2 companions from World history. Like I stated previously, I'm not going into a lot of details. If you want all the details you can go and look it up and find out for yourself. By know means would I want anyone to take my word for it. All I'm trying to do at this point is to get everyone to start realizing that these 2 companions are real and they are with us all and there is no escaping them.

Now I want to look at some biblical history of the impacts, or outcomes, or results of these 2 companions had on some people and nations in the bible. What would've happened if Abraham and Sarah would have choose to wait a little longer on God to fulfill the Promise he made to them about a Son. They instead grew impatient after a while and choose to take matters into their own hands. Abraham in agreement with his wife Sarah took one of his wife's maid servants and laid with here and she became pregnant and bore Abraham a son but it was not the son that God had promised. Once again companion 1 presented all the choices right and wrong. Once again companion 2 brought about the consequences from the choices that were made. The ultimate consequences all the trouble going on in the Middle East amongst all the different people over there and it's having a tremendous impact on the whole world even to this very day just like God said it would. There is no escaping these 2 companions.

What would've happened if King David would have choose not to go home to his palace while at war with Israel enemies and would have stayed and with his army and lead them. Instead he went home saw a woman taking a bath from the roof of his palace and lusted after her even after he found out that she was the wife of one of his generals. He sent for her bible says he seduced her laid with her she got pregnant. That lead to David trying to cover it up when that didn't work it lead David to commit murder of the womans husband all this took place in the sight of God. A man the bible describes as a man after God's own heart. Once again companion 1 presented all the choices right and wrong. Once again companion 2 brought about the consequences of the choices that were made. Ultimately the consequences were David lost the throne and his own sons tried to kill him for years he was on the run from his own sons. Because of the choices David made some of his people had to die their blood was on his hands in the sight of God. Read the bible if you want to know the whole story.

What would've happened if Adam and Eve would have chosen to obey God and not to eat of the 1 tree in the garden that God told not to. What would've happened if Adam would have stood up to Satan and told him What God had said about not eating from the tree? Adam was there when Satan was tempting and deceiving Eve. Adam chose to do nothing or say anything. What would've happened if Eve had chosen not to believe Satan and his lies. Once again companion 1 presented all the choices to them both right and wrong. Once again companion 2 brought about the consequences from the choices that were made. The ultimate consequence is that sin was introduced into the world and that sin cursed the planet the universe and every living thing. Now we get sick, have wars, pestilence, famine, and we have to die, and the worst consequence of all that sin separates us from God and we have no relationship with our creator and Father and it put us in debt to him. A debt we cannot pay!!! God had to give up his only Begotten Son to pay that Debt for us. Which brings about this question where does that leave us? It leaves us with a choice we have to make. Do we accept the only provision God gave us or; do we not accept it and let God see us the people that Murdered his only begotten son that he loved more than anything in the universe? I hope everyone is seeing what I mean by now about the 2 companions there is no escape from these 2. These 2 companions are everywhere and are there in everything and they have no limits. They never sleep, eat, drink, they never get sick, never grow old they never die. They don't even have to go to the bathroom. As you can see they have been around along time and they are able to be with everyone, everywhere, all the time day and night. 24/7 365 days a year. They will still be around when I'm dead and gone and forgotten about. These were some Biblical example of some people and history the bible shows about these 2 companions

Chapter 5
EVERYONE HAS TO DEAL WITH 2 COMPANIONS

Now it doesn't matter who you are. Where you are. What the color of your skin or the language you speak. It doesn't what you wear if you are rich or poor, healthy or sick, young or old, you will have to deal with these 2 companions. We all do each and every minute of every day and night 365 days a year.

Weather your a president, a king, a working man, a son, a daughter, a mom, a dad, a homeless person in the street. You will have to deal with these 2 companions. There is no escape from these 2 companions. You will never rid yourself from them. No matter what you do, what you say, or where you go they will always be there.

Now over the years I have met and talked to countless people from all over the world, and what I have observed with all their problems they have weather it be financial, health, relationships, family, drugs, etc. All the problems they have myself included is because of the 2 companions. The results or consequences of bad or wrong choices they made. Yeah you can try to live in denial; or try to come up with some kind of logical explanation for the problems. You can do what most people do that I've notice including myself you can play the blame game try to say to yourself and others that you made that particular choice because of what happened or because of what somebody else said or done. The truth of the matter or as some would say the bottom line is this. You had to make a choice and companion1 was there and he presented you a vast variety of different choices to make. Out of all the choices he offered you there is only on right choice or good choice all the other choices are wrong or bad. Guess what companion2 is there to ready to pour out the consequences or results of the choice you made that companion1 presented you. I tell you these 2 companions will drive you out of your mind. And if you did literally where to go out of your mind the 2 companions would still be there. Trust me they won't let you off that easy.

Now all the people I have observed and talked to and met over the years. I have only spoke to a few that were lying to themselves and others by trying to tell me and others that they never have to make choices and they never have any consequences. What make believe world do they live in evidently they don't live in the real world and the one they live in is a perfect one. No matter who you are, you have to deal with these 2 companions.

The 2 companions even affect us when other people make choices. Like for example our President and government makes choices on laws. What ever there choices are it affects our whole country and everyone in some form or another. So yes you will have to deal with these 2 companions regardless of who you are. One thing is for certain with these 2 companions for every choice that companion 1 presents it will always be followed up by a consequence from companion 2. There is nobody exempt from this. If there truly is some human being out there anywhere on the planet who is exempt; and who really truly never has to make choices and deal with no consequences. I really want to meet them, I give up everything I know and own to meet with them. I know I will never have to worry about that because there isn't.

So there we have it the truth of the matter. Everyone has to and will deal with these 2 companions. That brings about another question that is. How do we deal with these 2 companions? They are with us in everything we do. When we sleep, eat, take a shower, work, school, wake up, get married, have kids, they are even there when we go to the bathroom. They are with us everywhere we go. The north, south, east, west, the air, sea, land, and water. They are with in every situation and circumstance good, bad, sad, mad, happy. So how do we deal with these 2 companions? They are with us 7 days a week, 24 hours a day, 365 days a year, year after year, day by day, month by month, every second of every day. From the time we are born to the time we die. So how do we deal with these 2 companions?

You can't get rid of them like a house guest that has overstayed their welcome. You can't shoot them. You can't have them arrested. You can't chase them away. There is nothing you can do to get rid of these 2 companion. So how do you deal with them? Very wisely is how you deal with these 2 companions. You really have to give some thought to the choices you have to make. If you make wise choices you will have good consequences. That sounds simple enough right! Most of the time we don't give much thought to our choices we make we just choose. It's not until the consequence comes that we say to ourselves that we should have made some other choice. It's usually to late then to go and make the right choice or the wise choice. Lord knows I've been the worst of all people in this. I mean after all some of the choices we make we make in an instant like do I want a hamburger or a chicken sandwich for lunch. I already know what i really want and my choice is going to be based on my stomach and which one I like. I will choose not giving any thought to which one will be the healthier choice. Once again the choice I make even something as simple as a hamburger or a chicken sandwich for lunch will have a consequence sooner or later. You and I can try all we want and any way we want to escape these 2 companions but to no prevail it not going to happen. You and I have to deal with them.

Chapter 6
WHAT AFFECTS
THE CHOICES AND
THE CONSEQUENCES
THAT COME

Well as you can see by now the 2 companions are here to stay with every human being on the face of this God given green earth. So we have to make choices and we have to deal with the consequences of the choices we make. Is there anything that affects the choices we make and the consequences that come. Once again I'm no expert on this just another human being like everyone else. And once again all this is based on my own observations and personal experience over the years of my life.

From what I have observed over the years, and what I've seen. There seems to be a lot of things that affects our choices we make. Here are a few examples of the things i have observed. Our environment what going on around us weather its the weather, neighborhood we live in, or maybe what happening to our family or relationships or friends our environment seems to affect our choices. A lot of the time we make a choice in response to what is going on in our environment.

Another thing I've observed is our circumstances. We make a lot of choices depending on what our circumstances are or what kind of situation we happen to find ourselves in. The choice is usually made as reactions to the circumstance or situation that has happened. The thing I've observed about these kind of choices is that like our circumstances or situations we will change or choices according to the changes in our circumstances or situation.

I'm just going to name a few more examples of things that affect our choices we make for the sake of time. I don't really want to go into detail that much on some of these. The reason being is there is one of these things i really want to elaborate on in this chapter. Some other things that affect our choices is culture, belief, emotions, our feelings, or how we feel about something we or doing, and how we want others to feel about it, world view, faith, etc. Just to name a few. There is a long list of different things that affect our choices we make and the consequences that follow those choices. Perhaps in another book Lord willing but not in this one.

The one thing that affects our choices we make most of all is influence. All the things I mentioned above is influencing or choices in some shape or fashion. Everywhere you go and everyone you meet is trying to influence us into making some kind of choice. There are literally billions and billions of dollars spent on advertisements on TV, radio, newspapers, magazines, internet, that are playing on us and trying to influence us it to buy a certain type of car or truck. Or to to buy this particular product, or to get these particular services. Etc, etc. It almost seems as though Influence is a secret companion of the other 2.

You got to be very cautious of influence and not let it dictate your choices. For example why do you buy a vehicle in the first place? You buy it so you don't have to walk from point A to point B. Does it matter what kind of vehicle it is as long as it gets you there. Yes it matters to have the right vehicle for the job. I mean you would not want to have a compact car if you are married with 2 Kids as a family vehicle there might be a problem there. That's pretty obvious you need a family vehicle. What I'm saying is does it matter if it a cadillac or a ford. The one car is a lot more expensive than the other one and they both do the same basic thing. But the advertisements on TV for example will play up to your influence to try and get you to choose the more expensive vehicle. You know you can't afford the more expensive vehicle but if you get it people will see you a certain way. Your going to make some kind of fashion statement. Your telling everyone you are someone special etc, the list goes on and on.

Influence is a very dangerous thing or affect on our choices. Satan (the Devil) uses influence on everyone of us all the time. Look how he deceived Eve in the garden in the beginning. He used his influence to deceive her in believing that if she ate of the forbidden fruit that she would not die but instead she would have the knowledge of Good and Evil and would be like GOD. That influenced Eve's choice in believing the Lie. Yes there was a little bit of truth in what Satan told her but it was not the whole truth. Adam and Eve did get the Knowledge of Good and Evil but they by no means became like GOD instead brought the curse of sin onto us all, the planet, the universe. The 2 companions they are always with us there is no escaping them. If I could only elude them for even a min but I can't; oh how I've tried but there is no escaping these 2 companions.

Out of all the things that influence our choices people are the ones who influence us the most of all. People are the single most powerful influence on our choices we make each and everyday. Everyone from our spouses to our kids to our families to the people we work with socialize with to our friends to the people we vote for etc. I believe the reason for this is because we are around people all the time. But there again I'm not claiming to be an expert on all this stuff just sharing my own personal observations and experiences. So be careful and cautious with influence. There can be and will be some very dire and devastating consequences that follow choices made by influences. Most of the people that are trying to play up to us with influence to get us to make a choice it usually to benefit them and their appetites and their self centered motives and very seldom is beneficial to you. Once again who am I just an observer.

Chapter 7
IN MY CONCLUSION OF THE 2 COMPANIONS

There is so much more to write about on these 2 companion choices and consequences. But that was not the purpose of writing this book. Lord willing maybe I can write some sequels to this book. Also I leaving this book kinda open and incomplete as an invitation to others who may want to write about these 2 companions. There is a lot to be said about these 2 companions. What I have written thus far doesn't by no means give this topic just and it doesn't even touch the tip of the iceberg sort of speak.

What I do hope is that people who will read this book will start to give some thought to these 2 companions who are with us all the time. Also will hopefully turn to the only one who has all the wisdom for every choice that we have to make. We all need to really think about the choices we have to make. And make sure we are always making the wise one and right ones.

One choice by one person affects everything and everyone for minutes, hours, days,years and years to come. These 2 companions are incapable of having any feeling whatsoever for anyone. They do not know what it is to love, be sick, be in pain, to live, to die, to have compassion, mercy, admiration, or anything. All these 2 companions do is present us with choices and bring about consequences to the choices we make. They have all the choices right, wrong, hard, easy, complex, simple. They also have every kind of consequence good, bad, dire, devastating, short, lifetime and beyond. Consequences so powerful that they can bring down the greatest of Kings, Queens, wipe out a nation, bring pestilence, famine, war, death to millions. Consequences that can last forever. They can bring about consequences that can bless a nation, bring glory to a King, change a life for the better, bring about peace, understanding, etc. All these things can happen just from the choice of one person and the consequence of that one person.

With all that said how do you know if your that one person? The one choice you have to make and the consequence that follows may affect the whole world in a very devastating way or a very blessed way. That one choice may bring about disaster or peace. I mentioned earlier in this book that there is no escaping these 2 companions and how do we deal with them I said very wisely. The Bible tells us that The fear of the Lord is the beginning of Wisdom. The Lord also promises in the Bible that if anyone lacks Wisdom to seek and ask the Lord and he will graciously give it to them without finding fault. So that brings about this question where are you at today this moment? Have you made some bad choices and your dealing with some dire consequences from those choices do you feel it's hopeless and there is no way out. Well if you are, I'm here to tell you there is a choice you can make right now that will change everything for you that is to ask Jesus into your heart and life and to ask him to forgive you of your sin and he will come and help you and save you.

Once again the 2 companions are there with you companion 1 is offering you that choice and some others choices as well and that old deceiver is there trying to influence you on why you need to make another choice other than the one to except Jesus. The bottom line is you have to make a choice. Whatever choice you make you can be sure of this companion 2 is there to bring about the consequence of the choice you make. I will tell you this

there is dire consequences to not accepting Jesus Christ as Lord and Savior. The Bible tells us that all have sinned and fall short of the Glory of God. And that the wages of sin is death. The Bible also tells us that God so loved the world that he gave his only begotten son that whoever believes in him shall not perish but have everlasting life. And the gift of God is eternal life in Jesus Christ our Lord.

You will never choose to ask God for the wisdom you need to deal with these 2 companions if you don't know him. Because if you don't have a relationship with him you won't even care about his wisdom. Much less ask him for it. If you choose not to accept Jesus you will continue to make choices by your own understanding and wisdom which in the end is futile. Once again all I am is an observer. But thanks to the Lord Jesus Christ has given me some wisdom to share with others about these 2 companions choices and consequences. And thanks to the Lord Jesus Christ he has shown me the solution to dealing with these 2 companions in which there is no escaping. Yes I have to deal with them but through Jesus I can deal with them wisely.

Now maybe you think I'm crazy or whatever. Before you come to some conclusion about me. Let me ask you to do this little simple experiment. Go lock yourself up in a room somewhere or get off somewhere all by yourself. Make sure there is nobody around and and close your eyes and think to yourself I'm all alone. Even to the point of convincing yourself your all alone. And just wait for a little bit, maybe 15min, maybe and hour, maybe 3 hours. After a little while, guess what look over your left and right shoulders the 2 companions have shown up with some choices you have to make and some consequences that will follow those choices you make.

THE END

CPSIA information can be obtained
at www.ICGtesting.com
Printed in the USA
LVHW082010240220
648017LV00011B/325/J